'So'

'So'

SELECTED NEW POEMS 2011 - 2021

John Siddique

CROCUS

Published in 2021 by Crocus
An imprint of Commonword Enterprises Ltd
3 Planetree House
21-31 Oldham Street
Manchester M1 1JG

admin@cultureword.org.uk
www.cultureword.org.uk

Printed by Imprint Digital
Upton Pyne, Exeter, Devon
imprintdigital.com

ISBN 978-0-946745-39-5

British Library Cataloguing-in-Publication Data. A catalogue record for this book is available from the British Library.

Supported using public funding by
ARTS COUNCIL
ENGLAND

Some versions of the poems in this collection were originally published in the following journals and anthologies:

Perspective – *Poetry Review*

Nine Allegories of Power – *The Rialto*

A Specific – *The Journal of Commonwealth Literature*

Blue Water Lilies – *The Journal of Commonwealth Literature & South Asian Ensemble* (Canada & India)

Mauli Jagran – *The Interpreter's House*

Wuthering Heights – *The Interpreter's House*

One in The Morning – *The Interpreter's House*

Bottle Tune – *The Interpreter's House*

Whirlpool – *The Interpreter's House*

Winter Sea – *The Interpreter's House*

The Kiss – *South Asian Review* (University of Pittsburgh at Johnstown Press)

Fragment – *Best of Pirene's Fountain*

The Years Ahead Are Heavy – *Wasifiri*

The Last Skies of The Year – *Wasifiri*

Wuthering Heights – *The Yorkshire Anthology of Poetry* (Valley Press)

For my father and my son
And this moment between

Thank you for picking up this book, a collection of poems that I never thought would see the light of day. My intention here is to return to some of the themes from my first book, *The Prize*, but infuse it with all I have processed in the decades since.

The last two collections were very complexly structured, intricate books, almost novels in poetry in some ways, so rather than being on some crazy chase of trying to outdo myself, it seems more of a necessity at this time to return to the simple joy of creating a collection of poems that is more akin to an exhibition of paintings or photographs.

Where have I been for 10 poetry years? What happened? In short, I got ill and then I died. I died on the 14th of December 2014 in the ICU in Panchkula Government Hospital in India. And then without all that stuff you see in hospital dramas of electricity and paddles and shouts of 'clear,' I simply came back about 5 minutes later. I knew I was going to die; my doctor had told my wife and I the night before that I would not make it through the night. It is very interesting to know that you are on your last day. I invite you to maybe sit with this in your imagination at some point – how would that be for you to know you were in your very last hours? What would you do? How would you be?

Without going into the nature of what of are commonly called NDE's, near-death experiences, though there was nothing near about it – can I change the term to ADE's? i.e. Actual-Death Experiences – suffice to say, all the reports are true. After this and the surgery and years of recovery that continue to this day, I just didn't feel like putting books out for a long time. I felt like I'd said what I needed to, particularly in the books mentioned above: *Recital* and *Full Blood,* and a few of my literary essays, and that perhaps was enough.

At the time of writing this introduction I've had over 2000 extra days of life since that day. Imagine one more day of life when once you had none. Things don't look or feel the same anymore, and I'm not afraid to say that I use my time much more unhurriedly now. Much of what I used to value, including my reputation as writer and poet, mean nothing at all. I still enjoy them, and am very proud of my books, but next to holding my wife's hand, or being with my son, or walking amongst trees, I don't really have any great ego attachment to all the literary stuff.

The literary world has moved on and I've stopped being a somebody. Life is teaching me the beauty of being ordinary and real. My work as a meditation and sacred teacher is the most astounding thing, gently reminding people who want to know of the depth of their own lives, who they really are. I see all the elements of my life: work, family, the sacred, my books as one life in a lovely unique totality rather than being separate parts.

However, this book is not about dying and coming back, it's about life now in these times, it's about real things, real people, the impossible things we have to live with and through. It's about the beauty and the courage and the dignity of the ordinary. I hope some of the poems here speak to you, that they remind you of your precious uniqueness within the beauty of the whole.

John Siddique

EMISSARY

That my voice might reach you across the years,
through the pages of this book.

That I might share with you a message of
having loved this world, and the life from which
it all rises up.

That you may hold this book in your hand,
lift your own eyes, your own heart anew
as you step out this day to see the tree
before it is named as tree, to meet a stranger
before the mind judges and decides on stranger.

That my life might meet your life, and your life
recognise itself in all things, and in all people.

Love before it is named as love, across time,
across space, by virtue of love's infinity.

PERSPECTIVE

In the heart of the leaf,
the tree.
In the heart of the tree,
the forest.
In the heart of the forest,
a silence/not silence.
In the heart of the silence,
a door.
In the room behind the door,
a woman and a man.
In the heart of the woman,
a girl.
In the heart of the man,
a boy.
'We must look after the children'
they say over dinner.

ONE IN THE MORNING

All I can offer you is this night – black trees
against the sky. A road that leads towards home
or the city. Cassiopeia
      – a handful of stars through patchy cloud.

A night when we were both younger, saved,
      – cut from time to be lived tonight.

The rest of humanity has stayed home
getting ready for something we have forgotten.

I have never known how to measure the night
      – you have cigarettes to go by.
I know time and atoms - though neither can weigh
this branch against the grey cloud seen from below,
or the meaning of grey cloud against the deep.

The deeper we look, the younger everything becomes
      – all our nights reaching back into forever,

though sometimes a night falls back to earth
      – so we may see who we are now.

WHIRLPOOL

53° 4' 25" N   2° 0' 56" W

It rains hard all night, we stay up
to be alone together.

The town's two rivers swelling as they receive
themselves, filling up to make a big whirlpool
where they meet behind the primary school.

A beer can and a bleach bottle caught
by the circling, looking like they are going
to break free, but they are swept around again.

The difference between expectation
and reality has no syllable count.

The River Calder and the Hebden Water
become one name in an unequal marriage.

Away towards York, the Calder becomes the Aire,
though each was once an idea inside the rain.

LUNGS

A narrow path with water on both sides.
One side the river flowing into town,
the other, a largely stagnant strip: thick mud,
a beer can, decaying branches, a black bin liner.

Water drips down over red brickwork, the fading
form of something forgotten, over gritstone rock.

I am guided, or rather given no choice by the path
leading into sunlight. Trees on both sides.

The fine twisting ends of winter tree branches divide
down and down where the leaves will come,
mirror the passages and capillaries in my lungs.
The outside and the inside is surely no coincidence.

God In The Grasses

Grasses changing colour
A single stem speaking of life's sacredness
This moment
        - Simply being

REBELLION

53° 28' 55" N   2° 14' 22" W

In the aroma of coffee, surrounded
by Greek and Arab voices, sits a man
whose life has piled the stones upon him.
No one sees him, and he looks at no one.

Large hands take pink paper and a small
nail file tool from his backpack.

Folding in on himself, he does not reach
for coffee or water. He does not
look up or around.

Folding in on himself. No one sees
his engineer's fingers move delicately,
precisely, as if he were playing a Bach prelude.

Folding in, scoring, folding out.
Eventually he places a perfect origami rose
on the table, puts on his coat and pack, then leaves.

Amongst her books and her eavesdropping of
the glossolalia of the coffee crowd,
sits a woman pretending to read,
folding in on herself.

All her life those who have loved her
have called her flower. Closing her study book
as the tears fall, she goes to the man's empty place
to take the rose as a gift for herself.

GROUND FLOOR

We cannot live on the past, no matter
how perfect our rhythm was in those last days.

To live from the light.

To connect with others the best we can.

To stay connected – being loving parent
and curious child within our own bodies.

What a time of life to discover
the work that has to be done.

Watching cities of faces, each going
their own way, choosing to stay rather than go.

Not to flail against the darkness,
but to stay home and wash the dirt from
the ground floor windows of the heart.

BETWEEN BRIDGES

51° 30' 38" N   0° 6' 36" W

Light sparkles on brown green water.
There is something unreadable about this river.

The longer you look, the less
there is that can really be said about it.

Tourist boats cut and turn and dash,
as if there is somewhere to go.

I am happy
sitting on a bench,
amongst jostling visitors
– sparks before my eyes.

A seagull flies up,
winging from one blue metal pillar
to another.

It hangs around an empty rubbish barge.

There is something about gulls,
a mixture of vermin and spirituality.

When it flies, wings spread
as it becomes a coil between air and water.

It is the hottest day of the year.

An endless parade of footsteps edge
this north bank promenade.

How many miles do the sum
of these footsteps make?

Towards Waterloo, one bridge leads to another.

Horizon of new glass and St. Paul's.

A discarded chocolate wrapper
is animated into a dance by the breeze.

Water, sparkles, footsteps,
the spans of bridges, the seagull,
the sweet wrapper,
all want a home inside my chest.

They are some kind of forever.

Every sparkle looks the same,
yet it never is.

A baby in a red pushchair cries
from his deep lungs,
as his parents wheel him by.

Winter Sea
54° 29' 27" N   0° 36' 35" W

Great crashes of water against water,
wave against wave, against rock.

White water forcing itself high along the ramp of
underwater beach to explode against
the harbour walls.

We have come to this edge to watch the sea,
in the hope that water and wave can put
something in each of us back together,
wash the not flesh, the not bone clean again.

We have come to this edge as there is no
turning back the way we came, that would be
an unendurable defeat.

We have come to this place as there is no
path anymore.

The raging surfaces – wilderness,
but not so wild as the dive down deep.
An undercurrent, a movement driving,
sustaining itself across the earth.

Take my voice. Take my body. Take all the water in me:
blood, sperm, and lymph.

Take the intelligence. Take the bones, the gristle,
the meat and the skin. Take eyes, nose, ears and tongue.

Take the scent of me, and turn me to salt water.
Take the fatigue and the fire.

Take sex and hair, cock and balls. The channels
of connection: nerve fibres, chakras, and nadis.

Water against water. Wave against wave, against rock.
Neither water, nor walls, or words give way.

Still the dive down deep:
the marine light,
the movement,
the unseen travelling wave.

I look to you,
and you look to me.

No turning back,
standing at the sea.

The cold harbour wall.

A winter's day with
no way forward,
and no road home.

The sea is a blade,
a clean cut in the skin.

The curve of the earth,
the curve of our bodies,
old and new, and always.

Throwing our circles, our bindings into the sea.
Don't speak the unnameable.
Don't try to map unknowable terrain.

The sun rises in our east,
lifting himself from his dawn bath.

One movement arcing overhead,
the other great motion swelling below.

Oil rigs and electric windmills far from land.
A tanker steady and slow, tractors the pre-horizon.
Gulls gift themselves to the wind.

The name of the soul is not the soul,
fire and anvil, and water, and steam of life.

Body of water, body of fire,
trackless deep of oceans and space.

There is no path home my love.
We scream at the sea because we must.

There is no path home my love.
We love because we must.

ANOTHER SOMME
49° 54' 52" N   2° 16' 14" E
**For my Great Grandfather John O'Neill
who died at the Somme 5th September 1916**

We use the quiet before Stand To for shaving.
Before the fixing of bayonets, we make
ourselves clean. No mist this morning,
in the mud, barely a blade of grass to be seen.

Last night we moved from up from reserve,
a quiet procession, though the new lads puked
their guts from the stench. A lot of us here
from back home, from Lurgan and Portadown.

Sharpening my razor at the communal strop,
Sticking a bit of mirror into the mud.
Cold tea reheated in a canteen to use for hot water,
and a bit of soap saved in my pocket.

My hand shakes so much I think I will cut
my own throat. Standing in my vest, arms
by my side. It's going to be a clear day.
The first morning in a while where I can see
more than a few feet in front of me.

My face in the mirror, eyes do not dare
look over the parapet. Tom says he'll shave me,
shows me his steady hands. This is how you stay
a man here: be clean, mind your language,
look after your things, be a brother.

I'm unable return the kindness
of his brotherly gift. My hands, my hands, my hands,
just won't stop. I squeeze them into my armpits.

An old chair appears from somewhere,
Tom finds himself being the village barber
for an hour to the boys around us.
An officer gets the word and comes down too.
I'll not see that bit of soap again.

ANOTHER SOMME
(AUGUST 1939)
54° 25' 37" N   6° 27' 20" W

Steam from a man's breath,
grey/green as a field of morning fog,
he walks smartly through the room.
Uniform as new as the day it was new:
shoes, webbing, buttons and cap.

My mother Norah is a girl of eight,
cleaning the kitchen table for her ma.
Stops to see the familiar stranger
as he warms his hands at the unlit range.

Catherine, watches her father-in-law,
John, Johnny, stand there. Not a day
older than he was when he posed
for the photo that hangs on the wall.

He turns to warm his backside, though
it is only late August, and the newspapers
say there will be no war in Europe this year.

Mist fades to a green field, a field that
will never be Portadown, never be Ireland.

The Sun slants in through the window
at a sharp early angle. Norah watches
the dust motes dancing illuminated in the air.

BLUE WATER LILIES
In Memory of Sayed Bilal
31° 15' 18" N   30° 0" 55" E

In a room where no sound gets in or out
there is a scent of water lilies.
No sound must break the night air,
this night has been arranged to appear
to be just like any other night.

You try to live,
to not stand out,
not attract attention
but they know you,
they know us all.

They call you to Al Raml Police Station
to help them they say.
We become questions we dare not ask.

How many rooms are there in this world
hidden in the night?
Rooms from which no light may spill?
Rooms in which Sayed Bilal thinks of his wife
at home seven months pregnant
      she must be tired,
      she needs me to make dinner.
Thinks of his brother Ibrahim,
his mother who will have to receive his body.
Rooms scented with blue lotus
though they have never seen a flower.

A SPECIFIC
In Memory of Mohamed Bouazizi
35° 1' 60" N   9° 30' 0" E

Take your pick of these things:
A fruit seller and his stall
A city enforcement officer
A slap
A spit
The officer's certain smile

These things:
A no
A yes
A something in the heart of the fruit seller
A desperate moment built on all the desperate moments
An ending
A beginning
A can of petrol
A match
A shadow of a fox cast by the flame
A torch of human dignity – for all the desperate
    moments
when we are pressed, pushed, oppressed
And it seems like there will never be an end to how
    things are
And we deny ourselves, collude with lies and money
And hurt others and ourselves in the name of fear and
    belonging
And we cannot believe in change
And know there is no truth in the words of democracy
    and state
And we know there is no ending
            – we're just doing the best we can

And Mohamed says no, says yes, says enough when he
    is slapped
by a grinning cop one morning, who thinks she is
    untouchable,
who knows nothing of these things. Secure in how it
    always will be,
behind the numbers, behind generalities, behind
    bureaucracy,
behind the sheer lack of belief in our own hearts
that there is something in the human spirit,
            — a no, a yes, a reason, an ending, a beginning

MAULI JAGRAN
30° 42' 45" N   76° 49' 39" E

Slum town between two cities
where trains get no rest at night.
Where the first star of evening rises
to ask for your wishes.
Where cranes lift dinosaur necks,
moving steel and pipes and gravel.
Chandigarh and Panchkula's litter bin,
tinselled by foil snack packets,
and the snow of polystyrene thali plates.

Where the railway sidings call you
to go the distance into morning fog
to find boys, all with blackest hair
playing cricket with stones and sticks.

The world is full of beggars:
Poor ones reciting constant pleas,
rich ones with city towers of gold.
Turn down the sound on the television,
they all make the same face while
putting their hand out.

Mauli can't look you in the eye
without wanting a piece of you.
'Don't go there, you'll be killed.' I'm told.

Allahu Akbar sings out from the mosque
away down the railway line.
Muslim, Hindu and Sikh mouth along.

Mauli Jagran where the chai makers
and bangle sellers live. Heading out to Sector 17
on endless bicycles in dust and highway noise.

Allahu Akbar Mauli Jagran.
Meet my eyes with your eyes.
Meet me with only yourself
and your soul. Most everything else
in this world is not worth a damn.

I see a boy with a goat on a string,
a cell phone in his other hand.
I see a girl, impossibly clean and bright,
dressed to marry the day.
An hour moves differently here,
              - it is a syrup, clear and thick.
                    Allahu Akbar.

THE YEARS AHEAD ARE HEAVY
51° 8' 52" N   2° 42' 58" W

Full moon of July
                    A supermoon
The water in your body pulls to a certain emotionality.

Every day in Glastonbury
                    Outside St. John's Church,
the dispossessed gather. Washed up seekers who have
    sought

but not found.
                    Turned in on themselves.
No inner space left for a way in or through or around.

Drugs and drink,
                    once their freedoms,
wear their minds and bodies heavily.

The water of the body pulls to a certain emotionality.

On the close-cut grass, a hippy woman
          distorted by her lens.
          Her voice cracked,
          her vocabulary reduced
          to short syllables and sounds.

She plays uncoordinated Frisbee with a child.
She whoops and breaks the air
until the tea lady from the church
talks with her to restore the holy peace.

A hunched man with a tumour in his cheek,
      wearing a black rocker's t-shirt,
      crosses and recrosses the churchyard.

Under every tree there are pairs of people
who have come to a stop, yet their mortal years have not.

SUMMERTIME
31° 30' 00" N   34° 28' 00" E

We all bleed red, but which one of us is bleeding?
The sun and the sunset fall on all the living and the
    dead.
We think it goes on forever, but when the day
is done it is gone.

Cut apart the words on this page,
or a still from your life, find
the quantum spark of electricity.

Not because it does not matter, but that it does.
Not because of the bullet leaving the muzzle
to heat the air around it before it cuts apart
skin and bone to enter the chamber of the heart.

Forever falls into your bare hand,
trying to catch a feather or a sugar stealer,
or to stop bullets. When was a story ever true,
even when it leaves the mouth to heat the air around it.

The cursor blinks with the mind's grasping.
Knowing we all bleed red knows nothing.
Knowing every molecule of feather
will not make an eagle or a starling,
or empty the muted chamber lying
beneath the bone. Not because it matters,
because we heat the air around us.

BROCADE

The thread which warps and wefts,
knows nothing of gold and silver,
knows nothing of the brocade
woven in to make its outward form.

The wearer of the coat thinks nothing
of the thread which binds the cloth,
of the shuttle passing back and forth,
of the hands which fix the loom.

My mother's hand setting up the machine,
her bare feet in cold water, sound of shuttle
and steam. Not knowing the simple lesson
that the humblest thread is the foundation

for gold and silver. Power is forgetful
of its roots. Roots are forgetful in the dark.
The one and the zero
do not care to know each other.

A thread around which gold
and silver are bound in glory.

The fingers which thread the needle.
A needle passing through cloth.

To live one ordinary day and know
what it is to have lived that day.

The sincerest promise held against you,
a knife to your gut or your deepest wish.

The 'What if?' asked in a room full of certainties.
We live by the stories we tell ourselves.

The space between the words in this poem, or
the close distance between two pages of a book.

The accumulation of seconds in which empires
are born, gather their height, and become
broken statues and friezes in museums far away.

A whistle in the darkness, and I know there is hope.
Yes, it is dark tonight. No stars, no moon.
A whistle in the darkness, I have power over night.

Finally, love when it washes away the certainties
of a lifetime. When it breathes back more
than the world has taken out of your sweet body.

The difference between zero and one.
A zero placed on paper, meaning nothing
until the account is reckoned.

Meeting Life

With friends or in solitude
The heartbeat of life.
Heartbeat by heartbeat
        - Simply being

GATHERING

Outside - terraced streets
smogged in northern strangeness,
held in thankful anonymity.

In a 1950's front room - A single bulb
hardly lights where they gather, forsaking
the chairs for the safety of the floor.

Like everyone here, Young Siddique has been
carried on a wave of Partition,
a passport, and a promise of
'our home is your home.' A beginning.

The shifting gears of Empire's engine,
and yet they gather, we - the others.
Eating home food as best we can make it.
Telling stories of meals we would eat
if we could, not a word of holocaust
in this generation of holocaust.

Siddique tells of his mother's smokey baingan
and palak, the piles of hot rotis she would serve
from the earth oven, the cold dahi - made
that morning along with the buttermilk.
Strong flavours of smoke and green chilli,
hot bread and raw yoghurt.

The search for spices threads though Siddique's life.

That I could reach into this poem from
the banks of the Ganga where I walk with
the sense of him, sit him down opposite me
one more time and serve him his mother's dishes.

Breaking bread with my hands and letting the crumbs
     fall
to the table with the beingness and contentment
that is love. We eat every scrap, meeting each other's
eyes as men, as the natural movement of life.

Kasauli Noon
30° 53' 56" N   76° 57' 52" E

Looking down
on the valley of kisses.
Behind us the sounds
from the leprosy hospital.
In front of us – her past,
which we're rewriting
into present tense.

She is smoking, I am writing.
We try to photograph ourselves
in a series of inaccurate clicks.

Gum trees weep sticky tears
from chevroned lines
carved into burnt trunks.

A tiny old woman sits nearby,
simply being with the day.
Singing quietly to herself,
her name is the wind.

Evening Passage

At dusk I decide to take passage across
the lake. An unknown companion
sits in the boat not speaking.
The boatman leans on his staff, waiting
perhaps for one last fare, or a right moment
that only he knows with his sense of time.

Under these trees, on this shore,
with a red traveller's cap on my head,
I feel that which is in me and outside of me.
Not a belief, rather a knowing which comes
when all knowing is given up.
No certainty, not even in naming.
Something of each of us intersecting
through this moment, the space which allows
this moment to exist, and this love.

The boatman pilots us to a new shore
which looks like the one we've just come from.

No eye contact with the other passenger,
she is herself, dressed in white. I am myself,
not knowing, and this love is our wake
on the water, the pressure bow at the front
of the boat, the movement of the oar,
three people in themselves, three trees
on the bank behind us, and this love.

BOTTLE TUNE (NIGHT)

Our names are the high air
blowing across the lips of the valley.

A spirit-child blowing over
the open mouth of a glass bottle,
quarter filled with juice to make
a one note tune.

Opening the window to let life in,
to listen to the calling, it is my name,
it is your name, our neighbour's name too,
and it is nobody's,
just the monotone wind.

Whoever else is listening,
whoever else is hearing the call
there is a place in the heart of each of us.
Whoever else is deaf to the cry
       – a kiss to each of our souls.

Holy the listener.
Holy the turned away
the closed-eared.
Holy the high air,
breath of the night.

FATHER TONGUE

His words come out
instead of my own.

He in turn speaks
With his father's voice.

A great line leading to the edge
of beginningless time, leading
to the heart of the light.

Sword held high in Indian uprising.
Seed drill worked low in the fields of Jullundar.
Crossing the borders, crossing the story lines,
eyes that are not old see springtime.

My small hand in his large hand
as we cross the road in another country.

The boy and the man, the man becomes a boy.
I'll be sixty soon father. Your boy is sixty soon,
writing red lines for us all.

MOTHER'S VOICE

53° 37' 26" N   2° 9' 16" W

Desire and longing, to be loved
by a boy who never existed.

Emptiness carved out of her. Self-loss,
between the passing planes of war,
the sharpened edge of getting older.

A single enduring note of music,
seeking resonance in other women's voices.

Forgetting to remember who
she has been, who she still is.

There she is dancing in the kitchen
at 5 James Place. There she is
with sparkling secrets in her eyes,
black gloves and handbag on the table.

The music of her life
- the continuous tone singing on,
placed into context by the closed
parenthesis of silence.

THE KISS

We shine in the darkness,
under the quilt, behind our eyelids.
Arm moving over hips.
Flesh to flesh. Blood to blood.

Become one body in the night.
Skin against skin. Turning in
towards each other. A kiss filling
the darkness; meeting without

seeking. A kiss that knows
the source of life in both of us.
It fills the well, tapping the roots
of water from the deep ground.

CENTURIES

It is sleeting on the first day of April.
You are asleep in the room above me,
and I will wake you in a few moments
with toast and tea as I do
every morning of our love routine.

We pray for sun, we get cold sleet,
pray for blouses and shirts, and are forced
back into winter sweaters. We kiss
with half closed mouths sparing each other
the morning breaths that we have yet to brush away.

The pull of the day, working through Easter.
Daffodils and hellebores in the window box
outside - jewelled by cold glass baubles
of springtime. We talk so much but you like
to be quiet in the mornings, I'm full of plans.

Sometimes it seems there is only
you and me in this whole world.
Sleeping together, cleaning the house,
the joy of our anger, our rituals,
as if we have been married for centuries.

The Abortion

New life is just starting to come
to the cherry tree in the garden.
I stand behind you as you watch
the promise from the bedroom window.
Seed and fruit are the nature of the tree.
You don't speak. I don't rush you.

After driving the small distance
to the clinic. The people greet us nicely.
You want me in the booth with you,
to wait while you prepare.
Looking at the nurse's shoulder,
she asks if we'd like cups of tea.
I hold your hand while making
some joke about venetian blinds.

A tablet, a glass of water
            - a pessary, it is done.
The people are very nice.

Arriving home we sit for a few minutes
when we turn the engine off.
The closed space of the car.
The cut out tree against the sky.
A man in a blue cagoule
walking his dog along our lane.

Cleaning the kitchen together,
we do not name our loss.
You insist on cooking.
The flowers I'd ordered arrive.

As blood fills pads and cloths,
carrot soup and toast are served.

Shouldering your tears,
           - letting mine come too.

An inaccurate kiss, tasting each other's salt.
This is today; soon it will be tomorrow.

Repeat the daily acts of loving:
cups of tea, lunch and dinner,
fresh sheets on the bed.
We walk in the garden as the green
of the year takes hold.
You can have bubbles in your bath,
when this is over and done.

Into Air

An old pine tree, more silhouette
than tree, only its top branches
remaining, stretches from the mountain top
into air of eagle and sun.

The pine's silent reach extending,
by a few tens of feet, the mountain's
desire for connection.

Below, a few kilometres down
by the side of the snaking road,
it is cold in the sharp cast of shadow.

Children play running games in and out
of the gravestones in the churchyard
of an old Anglo settlement.

No one remembers the people
under the faded names, the day is awake
to itself. The view north is clear
for many miles to the snow peaks.

WUTHERING HEIGHTS
54° 31" 25" N   2° 33' 49" W

The pale face of the sun backlights the horizons,
though cloud overtakes her to paint the land
in edges, dissolves and promises.

Wind quickly changing everything:
heat becoming cold, dark air shifting towards hope
and lightness coupled with a bar of shadow.

The moraines of a house have been lifted
from the mossy grave of the moor, for tourists
risking their footing, climbing after one story or another.

Finding an unripe bilberry patch below Wuthering
    Heights,
we riff off the tastes of rough jams and summer puddings
    to come.
You sit where a young woman may once have sat
tonguing the corner of her mouth as she writes.

Her husband waits to kiss her soft edges
when she breaks into her wide girl smile, relieved
after painting lines of poetry into her notebook.

I kiss you too, as you talk of sheep and jam, aware of
new ferns unfurling from the death of last year's growth.

We are only upright against the horizon for a time.
The lintels of the house at Top Withens have been reset.
Weather closes in over us, over the body of the hilltops,
over the ruts of sheep-grazed valleys.

FLOWERS

You bring me flowers. No one ever gives
a man flowers, but you do.

Late daffodils and early opium poppies.
   Impossibly alive.
   I feel their living dying.

I don't own a vase, no one ever gives a man flowers.
I put them in a large drinking glass
with water and some sugar.

Looking at them on the dining table
after you leave, our conversation has
not quite rippled away. They bring you back,
make you still present. I love these flowers.
I close the curtains, keeping them to myself.

WOODWORK
53° 35" 24" N   2° 8' 21" W

The corridor outside the room is lined
with fluorescent strips, we queue
for this boy's only class.
Rabbling noise covering teenage silence.

The room is filled with the smell of wood,
the sounds of saws. I love the smell,
but fear the table saw, its shark toothed
steel wheel protruding through a thin slot
in its green metal box, waiting for the chance
to take your fingers away.

The room is at the back of the school.
The floor to ceiling window spans
the whole width of the room.

Outside the steeply banked grass acts as
a collector for our sweet wrappers
and cigarette end flotsam.
I wouldn't dare smoke near school.
I say we, but there was no we.

The teacher wears a blue apron,
he moves around his fishbowl freely.
I am tied to my station. My hands
will never do what I want them to.
The wood splits, PVA glue leeks out,
screws all go in at jaunty angles.

At the end of each term we take
our projects home. I slide my creations
into the house, hide them under the bed,
and never tell anyone about home.

DANIEL HALKYARD

You would see him in the mornings
walking around town. Stopping
at the organic coffee shop, putting down
his two carrier bags of shredded paper
or cloth, that at all other times pulled
heavily on his arms.

He was banned from almost every store.
Here they had a special routine for him.
He would wait by the door for his coffee,
putting the money into the waitress'
rubber gloved hand.

Sometimes he walked along our street,
taking the cuckoo steps up and onto the hill
to Heptonstall. His long hair almost
down to his thighs, dreadlocks matted
with his own shit rubbed into them.

But here's the thing – he was really beautiful.
If you could have shaved off the hair,
stripped away the clothes and the coat,
washed away the shit and the dirt.
He was magazine cover star beautiful,
strong and full of prana from the years
of circuiting his route with his bags.

He spoke to my wife once, just an 'Oh Hello,'
but that was the rarest of things.
I've never heard of him speaking to anyone.

I wanted to interview him, to make a mark
on paper for him: a poem, a story,
just his own words. Not my impression of him,
not this, on the day we learned of his death
this January just gone. A burst ulcer
in a hypothermic caravan lent to him by a farmer.

Every town has its layers.
You don't notice them at first amid
the funky shops, the café lifestyle.
After the tourists go home, we're just a small town.
Somehow that curse and blessing also means
that there is a kind of love, for someone
who is part of the fabric,
who is grit and yellow stone.

Layers, love, ignorance, mental disturbance.
There is grudging acceptance, and the missing
of a filthy beautiful man.

Blessings of shit, blessings of walking,
blessings of madness, blessings of hills,
blessings of coffee shops, blessings of carrier bags.
Bless us all Daniel Halkyard.

Before Thought

In every action there is:
Thought & Feeling, Form and Formlessness
Do not miss the reality of things
    - Simply Being

ORPHEUS AS A CHILD

Everything is bright to his eyes.
The spaces between the connections of life,

each sound is music, whether it is
factory thrum, or spider web vibration.

He loves raindrops falling into puddles,
tiny ripples, reflected skies,

rocky outcrops and tree silhouettes
outlined against the light.

(The sun reminds him of his father,
both powerful and distant simultaneously).

He dances in rainstorms, dances with the thunder,
loves blue and grey equally, without reservation.

The loneliest hills surrounding his early life
burst with different colours every day,
as the grasses ripen and die,
and the sun goes 'round the earth.

The purples of autumn, the gold of winter,
the dark black of spring,
the rapid confusion of summer.

Using his difference to learn about people,
landscape and birds are not enough for a life.
He keeps his mouth quiet, his heart open,
he holds each moment's hand.

Daring in friendship and love, though he is told
that he is too extreme: he thinks too much,
feels too much, speaks too openly,
loves too passionately.

He spent his days thus, and spends his moments
like this still. Seeing what is real, writing
the best words he can. Placing them into
the music of a line, creating a verse
in the song of the life of these times.

Last Skies of The Year
52° 57' 30" N   8° 38' 53" E

Here in the northern forest, December skies
are lit with cold sun. The shadows are long fingers,
but their reach is just beginning to shorten,
as we count to New Year, count our blessings
and our curses. Rain is predicted
for early afternoon.

There are long lines of track through the forest,
on which you will not meet another person.
Long telegraph lines bring communications
to the few houses, the people who choose
to be beyond the city's reach.

Overhead, long streaks of clouds billowing white
from a child's paintbrush dipped into clean water.

Painting

A child's paintbrush dipped into water,
the glass jar holds thoughts of what next.

The moment between the selection,
and the movement of the hand.

Wetness of paint on paper,
something outside moves to the inside.

Something inside moves outwards.
Painting and child emerge together.

A flowing pair of lines make a path,
white sheep are outlined with black.

The river is bright blue, swifts
dart over the waters and the houses.

Inside the main house is the idea
of the farmer, the child's father.

He has a moustached happy face.
The mother is a feeling in another room.

It's a clouded sky with mottled hills.
The sun will be in the next painting.

Rose

The sun is a painting. The child walks home
in the afternoon light of late spring,
or early summer. Schoolbag at his side,
heavy but not heavy with reading.

He sees the reddest flower in the breathing light,
and for a second, a lifetime:
air, sun, flower, schoolbag, and boy.

Looking closer he sees the flower is
a crushed-up Coke can, and life shines in him
as he accepts this gift from the God of all things.

FROM HERE

Accepting the gifts of the God of all things,
I rise with the sun and sleep when she is gone.

Every morning keeping a record,
a log of days, black ink on cream paper.

Counting the days, bearing witness.
Some days I am a man on a desert island.

Counting. Finding meaning
in the unspoken relationships.

On the next street the dog who barks all day
yaps its lack automatically, never winding down.

Watering the garden, it is autumn tomorrow.
The leaves are heavy, threatening to fall.

I go to the coffee shop where I will flirt with
the waitress who brings me toast and coffee.

VOICES

All but the last leaves have fallen.
The dark stone of the street is brightened
with small sheets of fading gold.

There is, perhaps, thunder in the distance,
or the voices of those who are no longer
part of our lives, but will always be bound
to us outside of reason.

You have taught yourself to speak
with your own voice. Their journey
is theirs, and this one is yours.

Thunder cannot be pushed away
by resistance or by fear.
The leaves have fallen, and soon
the year will turn.

You are already home.

Trees do not fear the weather.
All is part of everything.

Today, just like yesterday, the work is
learning to live the truth of love.

It Might

Brown horse behind the houses, standing in
the winter air. Bare trees lift up their branches
as signal catchers, as aerials.

It has snowed, and more might be on the way.

Quiet river moves and does not move.
Horse is deep in sleep or horse thought.
Everything existing all at the same time.
The fields roll away as hills.

So

For lack of love the world is dying.
We are unconscious of and separated
from each other.

Love is not to be found in the mind,
yet it can illuminate it.

Love may be in your heart.
The heart is both a vessel of
unconsciousness and of light.

Love is the active principle of your spirit.

So listen and love and act from spirit,
then look at your brothers and sisters:
people, animals, and plants.
Listen to the Earth in spirit.

Sacredness is not mooning around
in a special way - let sacredness use
your talents and identity.

It is an open hand in motion,
tending to what is truly needed
in the here and now.

CROCODILE

She unwinds the bandage
revealing her unhealed stomach wound.

There was nothing left to do,
but for her to put her hand inside herself.

Fingers inching towards the trouble,
withdrawing a small living crocodile
who had swallowed the moon.

She removes the grave of a sea captain,
and finally, the thing which had been
worrying her for so long.

A simple wooden flower
which she places at the foot of a tree
as an offering to Shiva.

FRAGMENT

Love and death are never expected,
nothing is the same afterwards,
all that came before, all that follows
       is only time.

Love and life.
We are bracketed by time.
So much emptiness surrounding us,
uncountable words in the mind.

You must exist.
       How could you not?
I had dreamed, thought, and spoken
the possibility of you all my life.

Other women came in your disguise,
sent as a test; I am no good at tests.

I began to doubt your existence,
deliberately forgot your name,
       became cheap.
Dressed well, beautifully.
O the heart without love.

Words suddenly light in the mind.
Love and death can arrive at any moment.
A savour running through all things,
the taste of them in our mouths all our lives.

Desire knows the meaning of time.
Love and life are surrounded by silence.
Half-words trying to resolve themselves.

WHILE WALKING

Trees are my friends
Birds are my friends
The river is my friend

The heart within the heart
is the sacred heart
The path of my life is the teacher

Tiny ducklings swimming on the canal
Heron in slow motion
Full green of summer leaves
The wind in the air is the call to prayer

We pass each other on the path
Who meets who?
One step after the next
Always becoming

The Breath Inside The Breath

Are you looking for me? I am sitting right next to you.
My shoulder is against yours.

You will not find me in meditation halls, nor in the
    mandir,
the masjid, the beyt knesset, or in the cathedral:
not in the words of a mass, nor in mantras, or sutras,
not in complicated yoga postures, nor in eating nothing
other than rice and vegetables.

When you sincerely look for me, you will see me
    instantly
— you will find me with you in the smallest house of
    time.

Tell me, what is God?

God is the breath inside the breath.

Kabir 1398–1448
(Version by John)

Sacred teacher and writer John Siddique has dedicated his life to honouring the authentic in our human experience. He is the author of eight books to date ranging though poetry, memoir, and non-fiction. His meditations and teachings are listened to by millions of people from every walk of life around the world. The Times of India calls him 'Rebellious by nature, pure at heart.' The Spectator Magazine describes him as 'A stellar British poet.' His writings have appeared in The Guardian, Granta, Poetry Review, and on BBC Radio 3 & 4. New York Times correspondent, Bina Shah says he is 'One of the best poets of our generation.' Scottish Makar, Jackie Kay speaks of Siddique's writing as being 'A brilliant balancing act.'

Siddique is the former British Council Writer-in-Residence at California State University, Los Angeles. He is an Honorary Fellow at Leicester University, and currently serves on the editorial board of WritersMosaic for The Royal Literary Fund.

www.authenticliving.life

Books by John Siddique

Poetry:
The Prize (Rialto)
Poems from A Northern Soul (Crocus)
Recital – An Almanac (Salt)
Full Blood (Salt)
So (Crocus)

Children's:
Don't Wear It On Your Head (Salt)

Memoir:
Four Fathers (Route)

Non-Fiction:
Signposts of The Spiritual Life (Watkins)